The Baby King

The story of Jesus' birth,
Luke 2:1–20, for children

Written by Gregory Hyatt

Illustrated by Joseph Qiu

CONCORDIA PUBLISHING HOUSE · SAINT LOUIS

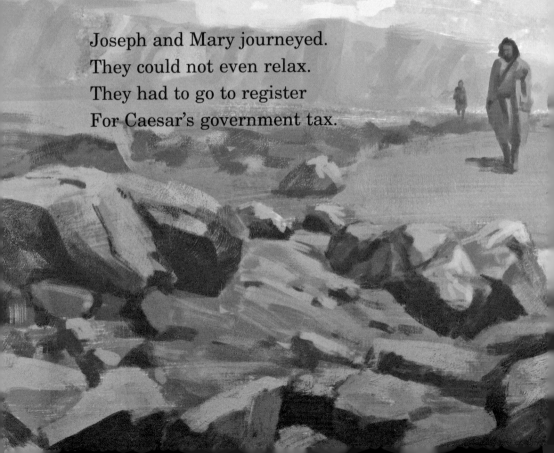

Thousands of years had gone by
Since Adam and Eve's first sin
When God gave them a promise
Of a Savior who would win.

Bethlehem would be the place,
Prophet Micah had foretold,
Where God would keep His promise
Since His Word the Lord upholds.

Joseph and Mary journeyed.
They could not even relax.
They had to go to register
For Caesar's government tax.

The trip had not been easy.
The birth would be that night!
But all the space was taken;
A stable would be the site.

As the shepherds watched their flocks,
Keeping the sheep safe at night,
An angel appeared to them
And God's glory shone so bright.

The shepherds all were awestruck
With quite an intensive fear.
The angel then assured them
And made the message clear:

They didn't need to be afraid
For the message, it was great.
God had fulfilled His promise!
They no longer had to wait.

In the city of David,
In that humble manger bed,
The world's Savior had been born—
Just as the prophets said.

The angel gave them a sign:
They would find a baby wrapped
In cloths, and in the manger
They would find Him as He napped.

The angel then was joined
By many praising God
And telling of His peace
To all who on earth trod.

The shepherds ran to town
And found their newborn king.
They praised God and told others
The news which angels sing.

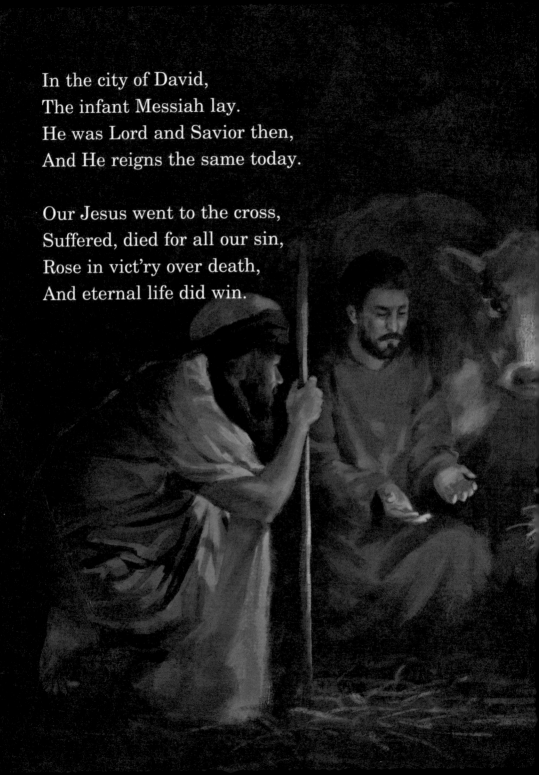

In the city of David,
The infant Messiah lay.
He was Lord and Savior then,
And He reigns the same today.

Our Jesus went to the cross,
Suffered, died for all our sin,
Rose in vict'ry over death,
And eternal life did win.

Dear Parent,

Many people go home for Christmas. They pack their belongings, get in their car or on a plane, and visit parents or other relatives. Sometimes this visit takes place in the town of their birth and in the house where they grew up. Joseph's journey to Bethlehem was, in that sense, a visit home.

Imagine that journey—more than sixty miles on foot with a very pregnant Mary. Joseph and Mary would probably have planned to stay with relatives in Bethlehem, including some who could assist when it came time for the baby's birth. But others had likely arrived before them so there was no space left. They may have been grateful for any place under a roof, even if it meant that place was a barn.

Imagine the shepherds on the hillside, bundled against the cool night air and keeping watch so their flocks wouldn't fall to predators. They were the protectors, providing a safe place for their sheep.

As you read this book with your child, talk about what it means to go home, what it means to have a safe place to stay. Then talk about Jesus' temporary home here on earth. He stayed here a short while before He suffered and died on the cross to take the punishment for our sin. Jesus' earthly home was not a safe place for Him. But Jesus rose from the grave and went to heaven to prepare a place for us. Heaven—with Jesus—will be the home that we journey to one day. This is indeed Good News!

The editor